YOUR KNOWLEDGE HAS VALUE

- We will publish your bachelor's and master's thesis, essays and papers

- Your own eBook and book - sold worldwide in all relevant shops

- Earn money with each sale

Upload your text at www.GRIN.com
and publish for free

Bibliographic information published by the German National Library:

The German National Library lists this publication in the National Bibliography; detailed bibliographic data are available on the Internet at http://dnb.dnb.de .

This book is copyright material and must not be copied, reproduced, transferred, distributed, leased, licensed or publicly performed or used in any way except as specifically permitted in writing by the publishers, as allowed under the terms and conditions under which it was purchased or as strictly permitted by applicable copyright law. Any unauthorized distribution or use of this text may be a direct infringement of the author s and publisher s rights and those responsible may be liable in law accordingly.

Imprint:

Copyright © 2017 GRIN Verlag
Print and binding: Books on Demand GmbH, Norderstedt Germany
ISBN: 9783668631373

This book at GRIN:

https://www.grin.com/document/411886

Lars Büchner, Mahei Manhai Li

Solving of issues with an ITIL framework, which occur during the shakedown phase in a software implementation

GRIN Verlag

GRIN - Your knowledge has value

Since its foundation in 1998, GRIN has specialized in publishing academic texts by students, college teachers and other academics as e-book and printed book. The website www.grin.com is an ideal platform for presenting term papers, final papers, scientific essays, dissertations and specialist books.

Visit us on the internet:

http://www.grin.com/

http://www.facebook.com/grincom

http://www.twitter.com/grin_com

Solving of issues with an ITIL framework, which occur during the shakedown phase in a software implementation

Lars Daniel Büchner, Mahei Manhai Li

Büchner, Lars Daniel, University of Kassel, Germany,

Li, Mahei Manhai, University of Kassel, Information Systems (IteG), Kassel, Germany

Submission Date: 31.09.2017

Abstract

Purpose
The research goal is to create a survey or a model, which addresses the problems and restrictions that occur during software launch projects. Especially critical success factors which occur in the shakedown phase. With that we want to test, if an implemented ITSM (Service Desk, Incident management process an problem management process) in a company can solve these issues.

Design/methodology/approach
To achieve the objectives stated before we created a survey (quantitative questionnaire). The results will be analyzed with a regression analysis or similar methods.

Expected Findings
Expected findings are whether or not an implemented ITSM can sufficient solve critical success factors or problems that occur during the shake down phase of a software implementation.

Research implications
One research implication is to enlarge the body of knowledge in the research field of software implementations in German middle-sized business companies.

Practical implications
Problems which have been identified in an IS launch can be addressed through key performance indicators (KPI) to monitor these problems in other similar software launches.

Originality/value
The value of the paper is that we will ensure that such problems won't occur again in future software project launches.

1. Purpose

The research goal is to create a survey or a model, which addresses the problems and restrictions that occur during software launch projects. Especially critical success factors which occur in the shakedown phase. With that we want to test, if an implemented ITSM in a company can solve these problems. The purpose of this work is to use a research methodology, respectively a quantitative research method. Main goal is the creation of a standardized survey which tries to answer the research question if an framework, which consists out of an implemented Service desk and a management process and an implemented problem management process can solve critical success factors, which occur after a software implementation during the shakedown phase in a middle sized company. These two processes are part of the front-end (Lahtela, Jäntti, & Kaukola, 2010). Out of this we can distinguish between two research questions, which have to be analyzed. The first research question would be to ask which critical success factors or working issues occur after a software implementation. A second research question is, if a given implemented ITIL framework can solve or defuse such critical factors. Referring to my literature review, a lot of research has done relating to critical success factors in software or ERP implementations (Yingjie, 2005; Markus M. L., 2004; Summer, 1999).

2. Theoretical background

Referring to (Markus M. L., 2004) implementing new software in a business company is almost like changing tires while a car is driving. Referring to (Häkkinen & Hilmola, 2007) a software implementation is a very complex project in which different stakeholders are included. Also a lot of issues must have taken into account. These issues can be e.g. that new procedures are not operating as expected (Markus M. L., 2004). Restoring business performances, which dropped during the software implementation is one major activity of the shakedown phase. This involves process problems, the managing of negative reactions and maintaining daily and normal operations (Ward, Hemingway, & Daniel, 2005; Markus & Tanis, 2000). As a new implemented software, no incident reports and just a few reported bugs are present (Peters & Li, 2016). To challenge these occurring problems one key activity can be referring to (Peters & Li, 2016) engaging users of the existing company. As well as the risk that a complex software implementation is failing is very high an integrated framework can solve these problems. I suggest an implemented ITIL framework, to solve these occurring problems, which occur during a shakedown phase of a software implementation. Furthermore in terms of a software implementation premature disbanding of the project team and training can be inadequate. Also operations can be disrupted and the termination of the techno change can be a snag. Deducing to these issues the main activities in a shakedown phase is the identification and analysis of these just mentioned problems and cleaning up data (Ivert & Jonsson, 2011; Ward, Hemingway, & Daniel, 2005). Furthermore operations are the rework of theses activities, which includes technical fixes and additional training for employees and top management (Ivert & Jonsson, 2011). Furthermore an ERP attempts to integrate all divisions in a company. (Somers & Nelson, 2001). In the ERP implementation research it is important to distinguish between critical factors, which hinder a software implementation project and which factors are not critical for a software implementation. Critical factors, which can for example hinder or delaying a software implementation are e.g. *"top management support"*, *"project management"*, *"use of* consultants", "project team competence". (Somers & Nelson, 2001; Summer, 1999; Yingjie, 2005) Referring to (Markus M. L., 2004; Fui-Hoon Nah, Lee-Shang Lau, & Kuang, 2001; Ward, Hemingway, & Daniel, 2005) a software implementation consists out of the four phases Chartering, Project, Shakedown and benefit capture (Ward, Hemingway, & Daniel, 2005).

	Chartering	Project	Shakedown	Benefit capture
ription	'Ideas to Dollars' – phase during which the technochange idea is proposed, approved, and funded	'Dollars to Solution' – phase during with the technochange solution is developed and technology is acquired or built; end when technochange starts up or 'goes live'	'Solution to Usage' – phase during which the organization starts operating in a new way with technology and the organization troubleshoots problems associated with technology and new processes; the goal of the phase is 'normal operations'	'Usage to Dollars' – phase during which the organization systematically derives benefits from the new way of working; may involve continuous improvements, 'upgrades', and 'conversions' of various kinds

Figure 1 The technochange life cycle (Markus M. L., 2004; Fui-Hoon Nah, Lee-Shang Lau, & Kuang, 2001; Ward, Hemingway, & Daniel, 2005)

In my research I address the third of the four phases, which is the shakedown phase. Software implementations need a lot of reengineering like adapting new processes to old processes so a company can act in their old successful way. (Amoako-Gyampah & Salam, 2004) Software implementation studies show, that critical impediments are likely to occur on reengineering and change management (Kim, Lee, & Gosain, 2005). Because of that, Information technology services should be delivered in an efficient cost manner, respectively at the most sustainable and efficient way to reduce waste and cut costs (Eikebrokk & Iden, 2012). Because of that, IT organizations, respectively IT divisions of business companies need a structured approach of how to implement and organize IT service management processes (Lahtela, Jäntti, & Kaukola, 2010). In this field one of the most used frameworks is the Information technology infrastructure library (ITIL) (Lahtela, Jäntti, & Kaukola, 2010; Cannon, Wheeldon, & Taylor, 2007). ITIL has become a very often used IT service management standard (Hochstein, Tamm, & Brenner, Service oriented IT Management: Benefit, Cost and Sucess Factors, 2005) the category, which is most important for this research work is the service operation category. The Service operation processes are dealing with the daily operations of an IT department to handle user requests, discover and recover errors. Supplemental the service operation processes are mandatory to ensure the level of service which had been bargained with the customers referring to performance or service level of an IT service (Suhairi & Gaol, 2013) As shown by (Eikebrokk & Iden, 2012) service operation processes are most developed in business companies (Steel & Tan, 2005). Two of the most important ITIL processes for this research are the incident management process and the problem management process. The incident management process is mandatory for capturing user requests and solving these requests very quickly (Zarnekow, 2007; Hochstein, Zarnekow, & Brenner, Service-orientiertes IT- Management nach ITIL – Möglichkeiten und Grenzen, 2004). A service desk, a help desk or a call center, usually captures these requests. Mostly with a ticket system, which classifies user requests with a digital number and mandatory information referring to that user request to easily identify this request in the future. After capturing the user request, it will be classified. Either it is a minor incident or a major incident. (Cannon, Wheeldon, & Taylor, 2007) This refers to the complexity of the reported problem. As figure 2 is showing, the incident management process is classified into the first level support. In the first level support a user request will be analyzed. The IT-department tries to figure out, if the incident is a known incident and the solution is present and had been solved in the past or if it is a more complex incident, which has to be analyzed from the second or third level support (Cannon, Wheeldon, & Taylor, 2007). The first level support team tries to collect all information referring to the incident (Suhairi & Gaol, 2013). The information can be collected through the asking of users or by analyzing information of monitoring or observation systems.

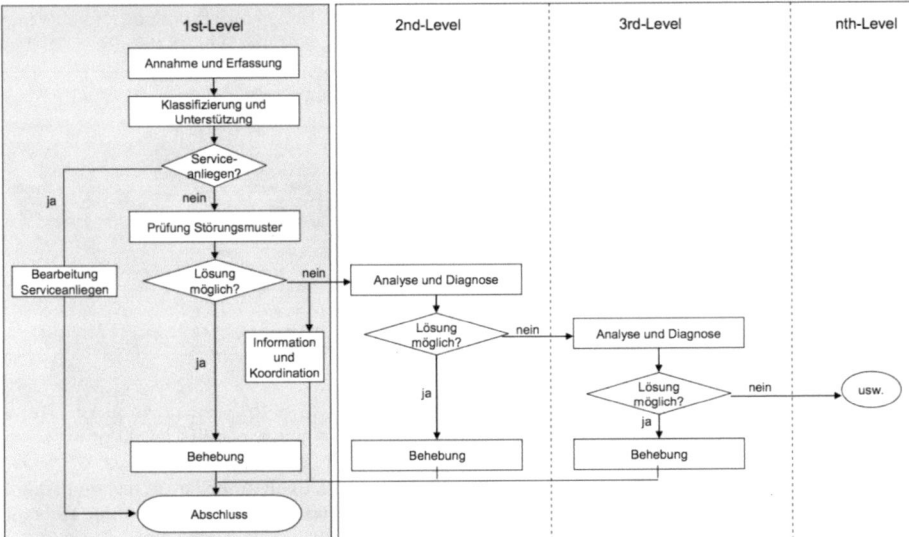
Figure 2 Important Service operation processes (Zarnekow, 2007)

If the first level is not able to solve an incident all information referring to the incident will be delivered to the second level support team. The same procedure will happen, if the second support level is not able to solve the incident (Zarnekow, 2007). The end of an incident management process is achieved, if an incident is solved and all details have been documented and the user who requested the incident is informed. Conclusively the incident management process is just for the curing of the symptoms of an IT error, which occurred during daily operations. On the other hand we have the problem management process, which has as a main activity the breakdown and analysis of the origin of an incident (Cannon, Wheeldon, & Taylor , 2007). Furthermore the problem management process manages all problems in the lifecycle. Additionally it has the task to minimize the impact of the incidents (Steel, Toleman, & Tan, 2006).

3. Approach

In this seminar paper a quantitative research method is used. I use a standardized questionnaire in which I want to test hypotheses, which are shown in statements, which the participants of this survey have to rate on a scale from 1 to 5. 1 stands for *("ich lehne ab")* and 5 stands for *("ich stimme stark zu")*. After that I will analyze these results with a regression analysis to analyze this data in a next step. Subsequently the results show, if the answers of the participants of my survey are acceptable and representative (Naumann & Giel, 1995). A linear regression is a statistical approach to analyze a given data set. (Berekoven, Eckert, & Ellenrieder, 2009) My data sets are the responses or answers to the questionnaire respectively the survey. (Raab-Steiner & Benesch, 2012) Distinguish between six methods to analyze results of a quantitative survey research. The methods are counting, judging, testing, asking, observing and physiological measuring. I use the method of asking. Because of that I created a survey, which employees from specific middle-sized companies have to answer. (Raab, Poost, & Eichhorn, 2009). For a standardized questionnaire concrete questions are mandatory to measure the specific characteristics like for example gender, age, customer satisfaction, motivation e.g. Because oft hat it is useful to use variable which have to operationalized. Another important factor, which is mandatory in a survey research, is the sample. (Bortz & Döring, 2006; Berekoven, Eckert, & Ellenrieder, 2009) Useful would be a sample of at least a minimum of 500 participants. Because of that the questionnaire will be send to multiple companies in Germany. Furthermore I want to figure out if an ITIL framework can solve occurring problems that emerge during the shakedown phase of an ERP implementation. In our research an ITIL framework stands for the processes *"incident management"* and *"problem management"*, respectively a service-, helpdesk, which gives employees and users of a specific software the possibility to ask for information technology help.

4. Data Collection

I contacted middle-sized companies from Germany, which had to answer my survey respectively the created questionnaire. I contacted a total of XX companies. The response rate was XX %. I used an online questionnaire, which every employee of the participated companies had to answer. The questionnaire was done with surveymonkey.com, which is an online tool to create questionnaires.

5. Results

Expected findings are whether or not an implemented ITSM can sufficient solve critical success factors that occur during the shakedown phase of an IS implementation. (Berekoven, Eckert, & Ellenrieder, 2009) Suggest a linear regression analysis to analyze if an implemented ITIL framework has a positive effect on solving critical success factors respectively impediments, which occur during the shakedown phase.

6. Research Implications

The aim of this research is to analyze if an implemented ITIL framework respectively an Information technology service management (ITSM) can solve problems which occurring during a software implementation. Future research fields in this area can be if an implemented ITSM can also solve problems, which occur around other implementations like a new study or working room or for example in a merge of teams or divisions. With this, I mean if an ITSM can solve e.g. communication problems, which emerge when these people are brought together. Furthermore it is interesting if an ITIL framework implementation can be used to optimize a Change Management approach, which is tremendously used in business today. Other research fields, which can be addressed through this software implementation research is for example psychology or human resource management. An important issue that arises during a software implementation is the users resistance to change. Psychologists or human resource managers could try to figure out why this resistance to change arises and how it can be overcome. The research implication is to extend the Information technology service model (ITSM) with a learning process. This research contributes to other research field like for example software implementations in huge or small companies. Additionally it conduces new knowledge to the research field of software implementations.

7. Practical implications

By this research, not only science can profit, also business. Identified critical issues can be monitored through key performance indicators or similar controlling methods. Furthermore it is possible to use this approach in other companies or business fields to analyze if an implemented ITIL framework, definitely solves information technology issues of the shakedown phase in software implementation projects or not. One implication for the economy is that, enterprise resource planning (ERP) software implementations cannot be initiated without occurring issues, e.g. communication problems, no top management support, poor project management, and so on. These issues mostly arise in the shake down phase of a software implementation. Also, these just mentioned issues contribute to the fact that science and economy should work closer together in such an information technology field like software implementations in a business company to close the knowledge gap between these two institutions. Additionally I want to show, that an ITIL framework can help companies to improve transparency and communication between employees and top management. Besides also the top-down and bottom-up communication can be improved in some circumstances by implementing an ITIL framework.

8. Discussion

To go deeper into that research method I will also analyze whether or whether not it would make sense to use a qualitative research method. Like for example expert interviews or guideline interviews, which are guided by an information or question paper, which the interviewer hands out to every participant. Furthermore it is interesting to filter, if a qualitative research approach would make more sense in this research questions. Additionally it is important to discuss if such a research approach will be depressed in a future work or not. For the use of a qualitative research approach speaks, the fact, that a software release creates different emotions in the employees of a company. Like for example anger or anxious behavior, because the employees don't know how to handle the new software. Because of that it is maybe useful to intensify such an approach. A useful approach could be an expert interview with such employees who are against software. These employees can be division managers or CEO's of a middle sized company, who cannot work with the new ERP system, because it is too complex and they do not have time to learn how to interact or use software. Furthermore because they do not even know how to use software, they will not push that software in terms of a positive marketing image or even speak about the new project management software. In guideline interviews such facts can also be identified. In such a qualitative research method a lot of other facts or problems can be identified which would not be identified in a quantitative research approach, like I did in my research. These problems can be for example a not sustainable programmed software which creates a lot of waste and other problems like crashing servers and so on. Besides because of a qualitative research approach, other research fields could also be addressed like for example business psychology fields or psychology in general. As a matter of fact software is used by human beings respectively employees of a business company. Due to the fact that, human beings are being focused in the psychology research field, it is very useful or important to do research with human beings, like in a standardized questionnaire or survey or in qualitative research like expert interviews or guideline interviews. Because of the fact that a qualitative research approach is often used in sociology or psychology I did not use this approach. My research area is business information systems. For that simple reason, I used a quantitative approach to show difference between these research fields. Additionally I used a quantitative approach, because in terms of software release management it is important to have as many participants as possible to get an overview and broad view of software, which will be implemented in the near future. Besides an expert interview has no standardized procedure and the results are very different.

9. Limitations

Limitations are for example the number of employees and that the survey will just take place in a single company. Conclusive the survey or the questionnaire has to be written in German and not in English because I ask employees which are working in middle-sized companies from Germany.

10. Conclusion

To enlarge the body of knowledge this work contributes to the theoretical research field of software implementations. With an implemented ITIL framework it is possible to optimize the communication between Information technology departments of a business company, which implemented the same ITIL framework. Like for example the IT division in Southeast Asia and the IT division in northwest of Germany. Besides the IT service itself can be optimized with a given ITIL framework (ITIL V3), because the five ITIL books are showing a lot of tips and tricks, how to optimize IT processes in a business company. Additionally long term service costs can be reduced with such a framework. Beyond communication channels will be optimized. Effective and sustainable communication is one major key to success in software implementation projects. Coming back to the enlarging of the research body of knowledge, it is furthermore possible to investigate this research field from a different angle. So, for example through a qualitative research approach to address also other research fields like sociology, psychology, business psychology or human science. Using expert interviews during the shakedown phase of a software implementation can image this approach. As a conclusion, one could argue if there are differences. So, if for example a quality management software implementation creates different problems in the shake down phase than an ERP software implementation or a project management software implementation. Another interesting question is what different issues do occur, if that software would be implemented in the pharmacy-, automobile-, financial-, retail-, biomedical-, or public administration business field.

References

1. Amoako-Gyampah, K., & Salam, A. (2004). An extension of the technology acceptance model in an ERP implementation environment. *Information & Management 41* , 731-745.
2. Berekoven, L., Eckert, W., & Ellenrieder, P. (2009). *Marktforschung - Methodische Grundlagen und praktische Anwendung* (12. Auflage Ausg.). Wiesbaden: Gabler.
3. Bortz, J., & Döring, N. (2006). *Forschungsmethoden und Evaluation für Human- und Sozialwissenschaftler* (4. Auflage Ausg.). Wiesbaden: Springer.
4. Cannon, D., Wheeldon, D., & Taylor , S. (2007). *ITIL [IT service management practices ; ITIL v3 core publications] : Service operation.* London: Großbritannien. Office of Government Commerce.
5. Eikebrokk, T. R., & Iden, J. (2012). ITIL implementation: The role of ITIL software and project quality. *23rd International Workshop on Database and Expert Systems Applications* (S. 60-64). France: Conference Publishing Services.

6. Fui-Hoon Nah, F., Lee-Shang Lau, J., & Kuang, J. (2001). Critical factors for successful implementation of enterprise systems. *Business Process Management Journal, Vol. 7 Issue: 3*, 285-296.
7. Häkkinen, L., & Hilmola, O.-P. (22. November 2007). ERP evaluation during the shakedown phase: lessons from an after-sales division. *Information Systems Journal 18*, S. 73-100.
8. Hochstein, A., Tamm, G., & Brenner, W. (2005). Service oriented IT Management: Benefit, Cost and Sucess Factors. ECIS 2005 Proceedings 98.
9. Hochstein, A., Zarnekow, R., & Brenner, W. (2004). Service-orientiertes IT- Management nach ITIL – Möglichkeiten und Grenzen. *HMD 239: Praxis der Wirtschaftsinformatik*, S. 68-76.
10. Ivert, L., & Jonsson, P. (2011). Problems in the onward and upward phase of APS system implementation: Why do they occur? *International Journal of Physical Distribution and Logistics Management (I Vol 41 (4)*, S. 343-363.
11. Kim, Y., Lee, Z., & Gosain, S. (2005). Impediments to successful ERP implementation process. *Business Process Management Journal, Vol. 11 Issue: 2*, 158-170.
12. Lahtela, A., Jäntti, M., & Kaukola, J. (2010). Implementing an ITIL-based IT Service Management Measurement System. *Fourth International Conference on Digital Society*, (S. 249-254). Finland.
13. Markus, M. L. (2004). Technochange management: using IT to drive organizational change. *Journal of Information Technology 19*, 4-20.
14. Markus, M., & Tanis, C. (2000). The Enterprise System Experience - From Adoption to Success. In R. Zmsud, *Framing the domains of IT research: Glipsing the future through the past* (S. 173-207). Cincinnti,, Ohio: Pinnaflex Educational Resources .
15. Naumann, E., & Giel, K. (1995). *Customer satisfaction measurement and management - Using the voice of the customer.* Cincinnati, Ohio: Thomson Executive Press.
16. Peters, C., & Li , M. (2016). Mastering shakedown through the user - the need for user-generated services in techno change. (S. 158-170). Istanbul, Turkey: Twenty-Fourth European Conference on Information Systems (ECIS) .
17. Raab, A., Poost, A., & Eichhorn, S. (2009). *Marketingforschung - Ein praxisorientert Leitfaden.* Stuttgart: W. Kohlhammer.
18. Raab-Steiner, E., & Benesch, M. (2012). *Der Fragebogen - Von der Forschungsidee zur SPSS-Auswertung* (3. Auflage Ausg.). Österreich: Facultas Verlags- und Buchhandels AG.
19. Somers, T., & Nelson, K. (2001). The Impact of Critical Success Factors across the Stages of Enterprise Resource Planning Implementations . *Proceedings of the 34th Hawaii International Conference on System Sciences - 2001*, 1-10.
20. Steel, A., Toleman, M., & Tan, W.-G. (2006). Transfor min g IT S ervice M anage me nt – the ITIL Imp act. *17 th Australasian Conference on Information Systems.* Australasian.
21. Steel, A.-C., & Tan, W.-G. (2005). *Implementation of IT Infrastructure Library (ITIL) in Australia: Progress and success factors.* Queensland.
22. Suhairi, K., & Gaol, F. L. (March 2013). The Measurement of Optimization Performance of Managed Service Division with ITIL Framework using Statistical Process Control. *Journal of Networks Vol 8 No.3*, 518-529.
23. Summer, M. (1999). *Critical Success Factors in Enterprise Wide Information Management Systems Projects.* Illinois: Southern Illinois University Edwardsville.

24. Ward, J., Hemingway, C., & Daniel, E. (13. May 2005). A framework for addressing the organisational issues of enterprise systems implementation. *Journal of Strategic Information Systems 14*, S. 97-119.
25. Yingjie, J. (10. February 2005). Critical Success Factors in ERP Implementation in Finland. Sweden: M.Sc Thesis.
26. Zarnekow, R. (2007). *Produktionsmanagement von IT-Dienstleistungen*. Berlin: Springer.

Appendix

Fragebogen

1. Treten vermehrt Arbeitsprobleme auf, seitdem die Software eingeführt wurde?
   a. Ja
   b. Nein
   c. Keine Angabe
2. In welchem Unternehmen sind sie beschäftigt?
   a. _____
3. Gibt es in Ihrem Unternehmen ein solch beschriebenes IT-Task-Force-Team (Service-Desk / IT-Hilfshotline), dass sich mit auftretenden IT-Problemen befasst, die im Zuge von zuvor implementierter Software aufgetreten sind?
   a. Ja
   b. Nein
   c. Keine Angabe
4. Welche Berufsposition haben sie in Ihrem Unternehmen inne?
   a. _____
5. Kann ein implementiertes ITIL Framework den Top Management Support erhöhen, sodass das Top Management die Software unterstützt, gutheißt, positiv davon spricht?
   a. Stimme voll zu
   b. Stimme zu
   c. Neutral
   d. Stimme nicht zu
   e. Stimme gar nicht zu
6. Kann ein IT-Service Desk Probleme lösen, die im Umfeld von Rechtevergaben oder dem User-Account Management entstehen?
   a. Stimme voll zu
   b. Stimme zu
   c. Neutral
   d. Stimme nicht zu
   e. Stimme gar nicht zu
7. Kann Ihrer Meinung nach ein implementiertes ITIL Framework wie es anfangs beschrieben wurde die Kompetenz im Umgang mit der neuen Software erhöhen?
   a. Stimme voll zu
   b. Stimme zu
   c. Neutral

      d. Stimme nicht zu
      e. Stimme gar nicht zu
8. Kann ein implementiertes ITIL Framework die Top-down und Bottom-up Kommunikation zwischen Organisationen und Abteilungen verbessern?
      a. Stimme voll zu
      b. Stimme zu
      c. Neutral
      d. Stimme nicht zu
      e. Stimme gar nicht zu
9. Sind sie der Meinung, dass Probleme die aufgrund von neu eingeführter Software in Unternehmen entstehen durch eine IT-Servicehotline entschärft werden kann?
      a. Stimme voll zu
      b. Stimme zu
      c. Neutral
      d. Stimme nicht zu
      e. Stimme gar nicht zu
10. Haben Sie noch weitere Einfälle, eventuell auch selbst erlebte Arbeitsprobleme, die durch neu eingeführte Softwares in der shakedown Phase auftreten können?
      a. _____

YOUR KNOWLEDGE HAS VALUE

- We will publish your bachelor's and master's thesis, essays and papers

- Your own eBook and book - sold worldwide in all relevant shops

- Earn money with each sale

Upload your text at www.GRIN.com
and publish for free